Franz Schubert

The conspirators: The household war

Opera in one act

Franz Schubert

The conspirators: The household war
Opera in one act

ISBN/EAN: 9783337197544

Printed in Europe, USA, Canada, Australia, Japan

Cover: Foto ©Thomas Meinert / pixelio.de

More available books at **www.hansebooks.com**

THE

CONSPIRATORS;

OR,

THE HOUSEHOLD WAR.

OPERA IN ONE ACT.

MUSIC BY

FRANZ SCHUBERT.

EDITED AND TRANSLATED BY

GEORGE L. OSGOOD.

BOSTON:

Copyright, 1883, by

OLIVER DITSON & CO.

HAS. H. DITSON & CO.,   LYON & HEALY,   J. E. DITSON & CO
NEW YORK.   CHICAGO.   PHILADELPHIA.

CHARACTERS OF THE OPERA.

COUNT HERIBERT . . .	. *Bass.*	UDOLIN, Page to the Count . . . . . . *Tenor.*
COUNTESS LUDMILLA, his wife . . .	. *Soprano.*	ISELLA, Maid to the Countess . . . *Soprano.*
ASTOLF, a Knight and retainer of the Count	. *Tenor.*	LUITGARD, CAMILLA.
HELEN, wife of Astolf . . .	. *Soprano.*	CHORUS OF KNIGHTS, CHORUS OF LADIES, THEIR WIVES.

"THE CONSPIRATORS" was composed by *Franz Schubert*, in 1823. The Opera consists of eleven numbers, interspersed with spoken dialogue. The libretto is by J. F. Castelli, a Vienna poet, born at the end of the last century. It is substantially a translation of the "Lisistrate" of Aristophanes. This is the first English publication of "The Conspirators."

ARGUMENT.

Count Heribert of Lüdenstein, with Astolf of Reisenberg, Garrold of Nummen, Frederic of Trnnsdorf, nohlemen and retainers of the Count, and with them many knights, have joined in the holy war against the Saracens. Their wives, Ludmilla (the Countess), Helen, Luitgarde, Camilla, with those of the other knights, mourn the absence of their husbands, and long for their final return. The Countess, irritated by the thought that her bushnnd, listening to the dictates of honor, rather than to the voice of love, could forsake her for so long a period, invites to her palace the wives of all those knights who had also taken part in the war. There, in council, she persuades them to assume a cold and indifferent demeanor toward their husbands on their return. Udolin, page to the Count, who had hurried home, in advance of the knights, learns of the conspiracy through Isella, his sweetheart, and maid to the Countess. In disguise, he atteuds the final council, and overhears the details of the plot. The plan of the Countess was unanimously adopted.

The knights arrive at the palace. Udolin betrays the plan of the ladies to the Count. The knights quickly resolve to conquer the ladies with their own weapons, and to treat the apparent indifference of their wives with even greater coldness. In the hall of the palace the ladies and knights meet, and on both sides the dissimulation is carried out to the letter; the knights, indeed, without so much as a single greeting to their wives, turning aside into the hall of State to hold a feast. The Countess is astounded at the conduct of her husband, and the other ladies now begin to find fault with the whole idea of the conspiracy.

At this point Isella arrives, and informs the Countess that 'nt, at table, had given as a toast, "War and the honor and had added —"But a short time remain we here.

Soon shall we take the field again in search of 'laurels. Meanwhile, let us avoid the society of our wives." astonishment of the Countess and ladies knows no houn This state of things is unbearahle. The Countess already c a secret interview with the Count. The other ladies also upon meeting their husbands. Helen first meets Astolf. Countess suspects her plan to have been hetrayed. amiahle mien she approaches her husband. He, scarcely at longer to restrain his feelings, saves himself with the impromptu story, that a fearful oath bound him and his comrades to return to the field. Bidding the Countess a last farewell, he withdraws. Udolin and Isella enter. The former confides to the Countess, how the knights in a certain battle, having heen completely surrounded by the Saracens, and with no hope of escape, had made the vow, in the event of their rescue, to enter upon another campaign; and that they would not allow themselves the slightest sign of affection toward their wives, unless the latter should don armor, and join their knights in fighting for the Faith. The Countess declares this they would never do. Isella takes a coat of mail from the wall, and dresses the Countess in complete armor. But only iu jest, as she explains. The Count here appears, and moved at the sight of his wife in armor, calls in the other knights. The Countess hastens to cast off the armor. At this moment appear the other ladies, armed cap-á-piè, and compel their leader also to remain armed. The men declare themselves conquered. The Count announces the discovery of the conspiracy. Mutual congratulation and rejoicing follow, and the lovers, Isella and Udolin, are united.

MARCH, 1883.

OR

THE HOUSEHOLD WAR.

No. 1. DUETT.

FRANZ SCHUBERT.

ISELLA.

'Tis he! O hap-py

UDOLIN.

'Tis she! O hap-py

meet - - ing! 'Tis he! O hap-py meet - -

meet - - ing! 'Tis she! O hap-py meet - -

-ing! Thou here a-gain, my U-do-lin! My U-do-lin!

-ing! O hap-py meeting! Of hearts that

UDOLIN.

love, how sweet the greeting! I am thy faith - -ful U - -do-

-lin. Of hearts that love, how sweet the greeting! I am thy

ISELLA.
faith - - ful U - - do - lin.
A
fz
p
fz
p
long, long year has come and gone, Since at thy
mas - - ter's stern com - - mand, For hor - rid war in
for - - eign land, I - sell - - a, thou did'st leave a - - lone.

6

UDOLIN.

And now good for - tune brings me home; The long, long year, 'twas hard to part! But quick my love, my long-ing heart, To dear I - sell - a bid me come.

cresc.

ISELLA. Hast thou oft-en of me thought? UDOLIN. Yes, for cer-tain, yes, for

ISELLA. cer-tain. Back to me thy heart hast brought? UDOLIN. Yes, for cer-tain, yes, for cer-tain. ISELLA. Nev-er

swerved, not once for-got-ten? Just as naugh-ty men will do?

UDOLIN. Just as naugh-ty men will do? Nev-er swerved? That's ask-ing wonders.

Well, but yes, for cer - tain too, for cer - tain too. Now, then,

thou? and thou? Has all been well? Yes, for cer - tain, yes, for

ISELLA.

cer - tain. Suit - ors bold, couldst thou re - pel? Yes, for cer - tain, yes, for cer - tain. In thy

UDOLIN.   ISELLA.   UDOLIN.

love wast constant ev - er, nev - er one al - lowed to woo! Nev - er

ISELLA.

one al-lowed to woo? Nev-er one? That's ask-ing wonders; Well, but, yes,

for cer - tain, too, for cer - tain, too!

Un poco piu lento.
ISELLA.

And each finds the oth - er the same as we part - ed, We'll live thus for - ev - er, for-

UDOLIN.

Un poco piu lento.

- ev - er true - heart - ed. And each finds the oth - er the same as we part - ed, We'll live thus for - ev - er, for - ev - er true - heart - ed; May

nought us di - vide, nor sad - ness be - tide, May nought us di - vide, nor

sad - ness be - tide, nor sad - - ness be - tide.

May nought us di -

cres. *f* *fp*

nor sad - - ness bo - tide. Ah !

- vide.

Each finds the oth - er the same as we part - ed, We'll

live thus for - ev - - er, for - ev - er true - heart - ed.

And each finds the oth-er the same as we part-ed, We'll live thus for-

-ev-er, for-ev-er true-heart-ed; May nought us di-vide, nor sad-ness be-tide, May

nought us di-vide, nor sad-ness be-tide, nor sad-ness be-tide.

May nought us di - vide.

Nor sad - ness be - tide, May nought us di-

Nor sad - ness be - tide, nor sad - ness be - tide, May nought us di-

- vide,

- vide, Nor sad ness be - tide, ... Nor sad - ness be - tide.

ALL IS STILL AND SAD.

No. 2. ROMANZA.

All still, and sad I creep a-round, My heart has lost its

power; How des - o - late my life hath grown, How still are court and tower.

And ev-'ry joy seems mock-er-y, And ev-'ry tone a tear-ful tone,

A tear-ful tone, Far,......... oh, far a-way, The light of my life........ is gone.

Ah, hearts which once each

16

oth - er love should never part- ed be, What seek-est thou in for- eign climes, Far o - ver land and

sea? If flow - ers blos - som al - so there, So

warm as mine ne'er beat a heart; Ah, nev - - er! Home - ward re- turn a- gain,

Star of my life,...... thou art!

CHORUS OF LADIES.

No. 3.

Allegro Moderato.

CHORUS OF LADIES.

SOPRANO.
ALTO.

With - in thy cas - tle thou hast called us whose knights are in a

18

for - eign land. And we have come, are now a - waiting, Most gra - cious la - dy, thy com-mand!

And we have come, are now a - wait - ing, Most gra - cious la-dy, thy com-

GRÄFIN.

- mand! Ah, be.... ye wel - come, no - ble la - dies. Im - port-ant things I have to say, And your advice would give me pleasure, And your advice would give me pleasure. Be

si - lent, hear me. Be seat - ed, pray! Our gra - cious la - dy

CHORUS.

shall be heard. Be si - lent, all, speak not a word, Our gracious la - dy shall be heard, Be si - lent all, speak not a word. Be si - lent, be si - lent,

Be si - lent, be si - lent.

Si- lent all, speak not, Be si - lent, be si - lent, be si -

Be si - lent, be si - lent,

-lent, Si-lent all, speak not, not a word........................

not a

not a word, a word................

.... word................

word, a word................

not a word, a word................

tr

Allegretto.

pp

p

COUNTESS.

Here is the list of all the invit - ed,

And have all come?

I do de - sire that all be pres - ent.

CHORUS.   ISELLA.

All,.... all,....... all pres - ent, Ha,ha!
UDOLIN.

Ha,ha!

pp

COUNTESS.

And one more than was asked, Ha,ha, And one more than was asked. I

And one more than was asked, Ha,ha, And one more than was asked.

hope that no faith-less trait - or, By stra - ta - gem en-tró has won.

CHORUS.

No, no, no - - one.

UDOLIN; (*Embarrassed and lightly to Isella.*) ISELLA. (*Lightly to him.*)

Am I well dis - guis - ed? Yes, fine - ly, thou'lt be

COUNTESS.

known by none. Does part - - ing from the

24

one ye love, Your hearts like mine.... to sad - ness move?

CHORUS.

We can - not dis - sem - ble, With weep - ing we trem - ble Our

life, our life,..... our life in - deed is most for - lorn. And when night is fall - ing, Our sad - ness re-call - ing, And when night is

With beat- ing hearts, we long for

fall - ing, Our sad - ness re - call - ing, With beating hearts,
With beat- ing hearts, with beat-ing

cresc.

morn, with beating hearts,

we long for morn, we long, we long for morn. We can - not dis - sem - ble, With
hearts, with beating hearts.

p

weep-ing we trem - ble, our life; our life, our life, our life, our life is most for-lorn.

weep-ing we trem - ble, our life; our life, our life, our life, our life is most for-lorn.

COUNTESS.

That must be al - tered.   We'll conquer them,   at home they

CHORUS.   Must   be al - tered.   We'll   conquer them,

Must   be al - tered.   We'll conquer them,

must remain, At home they must remain, And nev - er more forsake us.

At home remain they, At home remain they, And

At home remain they, At home remain they, And

No, no, nev er more forsake us, No!

nev - - er more forsake us, No, no, no, no, no, no, no!

nev - - er more forsake us, No, no no, no, no, no, no!

28

Allegro ma non troppo. COUNTESS.

Earn-est-ly let us con-sid-er, Now the plan with which we burn; From the dread-ful strife of bat-tle, Let us try their thoughts to turn.

UDOLIN.

Haste, ye war-riors, to way-lay them, Hear your la-dies' plan so bold, Wo-man-like I must be-tray them, I can ne'er a se-cret

COUNTESS.
Earn - est - ly let us con - sid - er, Now the plan with which we hold.

UDOLIN.
Haste ye, warriors, to way - lay them, Hear your la - dies' plan so bold.

CHORUS.
Earn - est - ly let us con - sid - er, Now the plan with which we burn.

burn. From the dread - ful strife of bat - tle, Let us try their thoughts to burn.

bold. Wo - man-like I must be - tray them, I can

burn. From the dread - ful strife of bat - tle, Let us try their thoughts to

Let us

cres. f p

COUNTESS.

turn. Let us try their tho'ts to turn. Earn - est - ly let us con - sid -er, Now the plan with which we

ne'er a se - cret hold.

turn, Let us try their tho'ts to turn.

try their tho'ts to turn.

UDOLIN.

burn. Haste, ye warriors to way - lay them, Hear your la - dies' plan so bold. From the dread-ful strife of

UDOLIN.

bat-tle, Let us try their tho'ts to turn. Wo -man-like I must be - tray them, I can ne'er a se - cret

Countess.
Let us try their thoughts to turn, Let us
Udolin.
hold. I can ne'er a se - cret hold.
Chorus. Let us try their thoughts to turn, Let us
Let us try their thoughts to turn.
Let us try
fz
try their thoughts to turn.
I can ne'er a se - cret hold, a se - cret
try their thoughts to turn.
Let us try their thoughts to turn.
Let us try
fz

32

Ah, ah, ah,................................

hold, I can ne'er a se-cret hold, a se-cret hold, I can ne'er a se-cret hold.

Ah, ah, ah,................................

Earn - - est - ly let us con - - sid - er, Now the plan with which we

Haste, ye war - riors, to way - lay them, Hear your la - dies' plan so burn, From the dread - ful strife of bat - tle, Let us try their thoughts to

bold, Wo - man - like I must be - tray them, I a se - cret ne'er can

turn. Earn - est - ly let us con - sid - er, Now the plan with which we

hold. Haste ye, war - riors, to way - lay them, Hear your la - dies' plan so

Earn - - est - ly let us con - sid - er, Now the plan with which we burn, From the dread - ful strife of bat - - tle let us

bold, Wo-man like I must be - tray them,

burn, From the dread - ful strife of bat - - tle let us

cres. f p

try their thoughts to turn, Let us try their thoughts to turn, let us

I can ne'er a se - cret bold,

try their thoughts to turn, Let us try their thoughts to turn, let us

Let us try their thoughts to turn.

f

try.. their thoughts to turn, Let us

I can ne'er a se-cret hold.

try.......................... I can ne'er a se-cret hold.

Let us

Let us try.......................... their thoughts to turn.

Let us try

fz

fz

fz

try... their thoughts to turn, Let us

I can ne'er a se-cret hold.

Womeu-

try.......... ....

Let us try.......... their thoughts to turn, Let us try

Let us try

fz

fz

fp

fz

try, Let us try their thoughts to turn, Let us
-like, I must be-tray them, I can ne'er a se-cret hold. Woman-
Let us try, Let us try their thoughts to turn. Let us try,
try, Let us try their thoughts to turn.
like, I must be-tray them, I can ne'er a se-cret hold, I can ne'er a se-cret
Let us try, Let us try their thoughts to turn.
f

From the dreadful strife of bat-tle, From the dreadful strife of

hold, I can ne'er a se-cret hold, I can ne'er a se-cret hold, I can ne'er a se-cret

From the dreadful strife of bat-tle, From the dreadful strife of

bat-tle, Let us try their thoughts to turn.

hold, I can ne'er a se-cret hold.

bat-tle. Let us try their thoughts to turn.

THE CONSPIRACY.

No. 4.
CHORUS.
Allegro.

SOPRANO.

ALTO. Yes, we swear it!

Allegro.

pp

espress.

f

pp

Yes, we swear it! Yes, we swear it!

COUNTESS.

The voice of love, ye'll nev - er

f

p

f

p

CHORUS.

hear it? The voice of love, we'll nev - er hear it!

mf

p

f

COUNTESS.
Swear all your husbands to treat cold - ly!
CHORUS.
Swear all our husbands to treat
cold - ly!
p
mf
p
COUNTESS.
From love to indiff'rence changing bold - ly!
CHORUS.
From
f
mf
COUNTESS.
love to indiff'rence changing bold - ly!
No sup - - plicant be kiss - ing
p
f

CHORUS.

blind - ly? That is too much, Con - sid - er kind - ly! That is too

That is too much, Con - sid - er kind - ly!

mf

p

much. Con - sid - er kind - ly! No sup - - - plicant be kiss - ing

COUNTESS.

That is too much, Con - sid - er kind - ly!

fp

blind - ly? No sup - - plicant be kiss - ing blind - ly?

mf

cres.

f

p

CHORUS.

COUNTESS.

No sup - pli - cant be kiss - - ing blind - ly, Un -

- til they shall a - - dopt our plan? Un - til they shall a - - dopt our plan.

CHORUS.

COUNTESS.

We've giv'n our word, We will not break it; Nor when by sweet entrea - ty

We've giv'n our word, We will not break it; Nor when by sweet entrea - ty

We've giv'n our word, We've giv'n our word, We will not break it; Nor when by sweet entrea - ty stirred,.......... Our hearts would make us break our word. We've giv'n our word,

stirred,.......... Our hearts would make us break our word. We've giv'n our word,

stirred,.......... Our hearts would make us break our word. We've giv'n our word, We will not

fz fz fz fz *f* *mf* *mf*

We will not break it, Nor when by sweet entrea - ty stirred, ... Our hearts would make us break our

We will not break it, Nor when by sweet entrea - ty stirred, ... Our hearts would make us break our

break it, Nor when by sweet entrea - ty stirred, ... Our hearts would make us break our

cres. *fz fz fz fz*

word, Nor when by sweet en - trea - ty stirred, Our hearts would make us break our

word, Nor when by sweet en - trea - ty stirred, Our hearts would make us break our

word. We've given our word, we will........ not break........ it.

word. We've given our word, we will........ not break .... it.

COUNTESS.
Andantino.

Be brave! be brave! re - ward will come some day.....

pp CHORUS.

Be brave! be brave! re -

pp

Be brave! be brave! re -

Andantino.

pp

Now qui - et - ly let us a - way, Now qui - et - ly let us a - way,

- ward will come some day..... Now qui - et - ly let us a - way, Be

ward will come some day..... Now qui - et - ly let us a - way, Be

Be brave! be brave! re - ward will come some day,.... Now qui - et - ly let us a - way, Now

brave!.... be brave!.... re - ward will come some day,.... Now qui - et - ly

brave!.... be brave!.... re - ward will come some day, ... Now qui - et - ly

qui - et - ly let us a - way. Be brave! be brave! re - ward will come some day,....

'et us a - way, Be brave!.... be brave! ... re - ward will come some day,....

let us a - way, Be brave!.... be brave!.... re - ward will come some day,.... Be

be brave! re - ward........ will come........ some day,.... be
be brave! re - ward........ will come........ some day,.... be
brave! be brave! re - ward.... will come........ some day..... be brave! be
brave! re - ward........ will come........ some day..... Now qui - et - ly let us a - way,
brave! re - ward........ will come........ some day..... Now
brave! re - ward........ will come........ some day..... Now
pp

Now qui-et-ly let us a-way, Now

qui-et-ly let us a-way, Now qui-et-ly let us a-way, Now

qui - et - ly let us............... a - way...............

qui - et - ly let us............... a - way...............

MARCH AND CHORUS OF KNIGHTS.

Allegro Moderato.

CHORUS.

TENOR.

Now end - ed is this life Of hard-ship and of strife; Our

BASS.

vows per-form'd re -turn we home, As vic - tors for the Faith we come.

Rest now, my trus-ty sword; Let strug-gles fierce give way to peaceful

life and lov-er's play, Rest now, my sword; Let strug-gles fierce give way, To peaceful

life and lov-er's play. This i-ron coat of mail, Up-on the wall im-pale; For it is

50

meet that a-valiant knight, who has his vows perform'd aright. In rest should find, in rest should find, should find reward.

Now end-ed is this life Of hard-ship and of strife; Our

vows perform'd re-turn we home, As vic-tors for the Faith we come.

Now end-ed is this life of hard-ship and of strife. Our

vows per-formed, re-turn we home, As vic-tors for the faith we come: Now

end-ed is this life of hardship and of strife.

CHORUS OF KNIGHTS.

No. 6.

Allegro moderato.

UDOLIN.

There is trea - son in the air! Treason in the air!

COUNT.

UDOLIN.

A lit - tle plan, I heard them

CHORUS.

What! treason in the air?

Count.
Udolin.
Count.
swear. Come, let us hear! Against ye all is war de - clared. What!
Come, let us hear.
Come, let us hear.
tr
f
mf
p
f
Udolin.
Count.
war declared? But not with swords be ye prepared. How, without swords?
What! war declared? How, without
What! war declared? How, without
mf
p

UDOLIN.

COUNT.

Aye, stra - ta - gy, ye need for win - ning. That were dis

swords?

swords?

mf   *p*

- grace.

UDOLIN.

Out of your weak - ness they a plan were spin -

That were disgrace.

That were disgrace.

p

COUNT.
UDOLIN.
COUNT.
-ning. We're not a weak race.
And know ye who these reb - els are?
We
We're not, no, no!
We're not, no, no!
f
p
know it not.
UDOLIN.
And know ye who these reb - les are?
COUNT.
We know it not!
We know it not.
We know it
We know it not.
We know it

Udolin.
Count.
Your la - dies, your la - dies, they have declared the war. How
not. How
not. How
f
they their du - ty have for - got, How they their
they their du - ty have for - got, How they their
they their du - ty have for - got, How they their

du - ty have for - got!.............................

du - ty have for - got!.............................

decres.

UDOLIN.

They held a se - cret session, Where all made one con - fes - sion. They had a

p

tr

plan to increase your af - fection, That all ad - vanc - es meet with re - jection. For a fi - na - le they swore

tr

this: They'd never al - low a sin - gle kiss, Un- til ye'd sworn and un - der - signed, That

ye would be re - signed At home in fu - ture to re - main, Nor take up arms a-

- gain.

UDOLIN.
Aye, they shall repent it.
COUNT.
Ha, they shall repent it.

CHORUS.
Ha, they shall re - pent it, And their fruitless

cresc.

f

p

60

Let us, com-rades all, Now al-ly a-gainst it.

Let us, com-rades all, Now al-ly a-gainst it.

Let us, com-rades all, Now al-ly a-gainst it, Man's su-per-ior,

Man's su-per-ior mind More than a match they'll find. Let us, com-rades all,

Man's su-per-ior mind More than a match they'll find. Let us, com-rades all,

Man's su-per-ior mind More than a match they'll find. Let us, com-rades

p

now al - ly a - gainst it, Man's su - per - ior, Man's su - per - ior mind; More than a

now al - ly a - gainst it, Man's su - per - ior, Man's su - per - ior mind; More than a

all, Now al - ly a - gainst it, Man's su - per - ior mind; More than a

match they'll find, More than a match they'll find.

match they'll find, More than a match they'll find.

match they'll find, More than a match they'll find.

Ha! they shall re - pent it.

Ha! they shall re - pent it.

Ha! they shall re - pent it, And their fruit-less,

And their fruitless plan, They will sure re - lent it, And their fruit less

And their fruitless plan, They will sure re - lent it, And their fruit-less

plan. They will sure re - lent it, And their fruit-less plan,

And their fruit-less

plan, They......... will sure re - lent it.
plan, They......... will sure re - lent it.
They will sure......... will sure re - lent it.
plan, They......... will sure re - lent it.
fz
p
Ha, they shall re - pent it, Yes, they shall re - pent it, And their fruitless
Ha, they shall re - pent it, And their fruit-less plan,
Ha, they shall re - pent it, Yes, they shall re - pent it, And their fruitless
Ha, they shall re - pent it, And their fruit-less plan,
cresc.
ff

plan, They will sure re - lent it, Ha, they shall re -
They will sure re - lent it,
plan, They will sure re - lent it, Ha, they shall re -
They will sure re - lent it,
dim.
- pent it, Ha, they shall re - pent it, And their fruit - less plan, they will
Ha, they shall re - pent it, And their fruit-less plan, They will sure, they will
- pent it, Ha, they shall re - pent it, And their fruit - less plan, they will
Ha, they shall re - pent it, And their fruit-less plan, They will sure, they will
cresc.
ff

sure re - lent it, Sure- ly, sure- ly, They will sure re - lent
sure re - lent it, Sure- ly, sure- ly, They will sure re - lent
sure re - lent it, Sure- ly, sure- ly, They will sure re - lent
ff
it, Sure- ly, sure- ly, They will sure re - lent it.
it, Sure- ly, sure, ly, They will sure re - lent it.
it, Sure- ly, sure- ly, They will sure re - lent it.

Sure - - ly, sure - - ly, They will sure re - lent

Sure - - ly, sure - - ly, They will sure re - lent

Sure - - ly, sure - - ly, They will sure re - lent

it.

it.

it.

CHORUS OF KNIGHTS AND LADIES.

No. 7.

Andantino.

CHORUS OF LADIES.
SOPRANO.

O wel - come, wel-come meet - ing, In this, your na - tive land!

ALTO.

CHORUS OF KNIGHTS.
TENOR. (*Aside.*)

welcome meeting, In this, your native land! No war-riors these we're greeting, No

BASS. (*Aside.*)

No warriors these we're greeting, No warriors these we're

CHORUS OF LADIES.

O welcome, welcome meeting, In

warriors these we're greeting. Now firm - ly let us stand, Now firmly let us stand.

greeting. Now firm - ly let us stand, Now let us stand, Now firmly let us stand.

fp

70

this, your na - tive land. Wel - come meet - ing, In

No warriors these we're greet - ing.

this, your na - tive land.

Now firm - ly let us stand.

COUNTESS. (*Aside.*)

How well he looks!

LUITGARD. (*Aside.*)

I'd like to

fp

HELEN. (*Aside.*) KAMILA. (*Aside.*)

know him. He's hand-som-er than ev - er, sure; That coat of mail it does be - come him.

A LADY. (*Aside.*)

He's handsomer than ev - er, sure.

CHORUS OF LADIES. (*Aside.*)

Of meeting, ca - ress - ing, How sweet were the plea - sure! 'Tis sad to be parted from life's dearest treasure, How sweet were the pleasure, 'Tis sad to be parted from life's dearest

treasure. Be si-lent, my heart, I'll heed thee no long-er, For sure is my

fail-ure, un-less I be stronger. Be silent my heart, I'll heed thee no long - er, For sure is my fail - ure, un - less I be stronger.

By Charles the

faith-ful, how fair she is! How to my heart her glances spoke! How long the time, and not one

ASTOLF. (*Aside.*)

FRIEDRIC. (*Aside.*)

kiss!

GAROLD. (*Aside.*)

This is an in - con - ve - nient joke.

CHORUS OF KNIGHTS. (*Aside.*)

Of meeting, ca - ross - ing, How sweet were the

pleasure, 'Tis sad to be parted From life's dearest treasure.

How sweet were the

pleasure, 'Tis sad to be part-ed From life's dearest treasure.

Be

si - lent, my heart, I'll heed thee no long - er, For sure is my fail - ure, un-

-less I be stronger. Be si-lent, my heart, I'll heed thee no

long-er, For sure is my fail-ure, un-less I be stronger.

76

fond. Play well your parts, All fear dis-pel, De - ny your hearts, And

fond. Play well your parts, All fear dis-pel, De - ny your hearts, And all will be well.

all will be well. Clos - er still, love ties the bond, Love op - posed.... will grow more

Clos - er still, love ties the bond, Love op-posed will grow more

fond. Clos - er still, love ties the bond, Love op - posed.... will grow more

fond. Clos - er still, love ties the bond, Love op-posed will grow more

CHORUS OF KNIGHTS.

fond. To the

fond. To the

p cres. _f_

CHORUS OF LADIES.

I'm as-tound -

Am I dream - ing?

hall of state re - pair, See the gob - lets glanc - ing, Where the

hall of state re - pair, See the gob - lets glanc - ing, Where the

_p_ _f_

-ed!   Am I dream - ing?

I'm as tound -

wind is so fragrant and fair, Pleasure it brings en -tranc - ing.

f   p

-ed!

Love is tame, 'tis a pi-ti-ful game.   When at war, At his wine,

CHORUS OF KNIGHTS. p

Love is tame, 'tis a pi-ti-ful game.

p   f

Not a

Not a

on his steed, | Know ye the knight by val-iant deed? Know ye the knight by valiant deed?

on his steed. | Know ye the Knight by val-iant deed? Know ye the knight by valiant deed?

word do they say, Not a word do they say, with-out a single greet - ing, They hur - ry a - way. De -

word do they say, Not a word do they say, with-out a single greet - ing, They hur - ry a - way. De -

Love is tame, 'tis a pit - i - ful game.

Love is tame, 'tis a pit - i - ful game.

Chorus of Ladies.
- ni - al is an ea - sy task, Our com - pa - ny they do not ask.

f Chorus of Knights.
When at war, at his wine, on his steed, Know ye the knight by val - iant deed?

p Chorus of Ladies.
De - ni - al is an ea - sy task, Our com - pa - ny they do not ask.
Know ye the Knight by val-iant deed? To the

I'm as-tound -

Am I dream - ing?

hall of state re - pair, See the gob - lets glanc - ing, Where the

wine is so fragrant and fair, Pleasure it brings en -tranc - ing.

- ed!

Am I dream - ing?

I'm as tound -

CHORUS OF LADIES.

Not a

Not a

.. ed!

Love is tame, 'tis a pit-i-ful game.

Love is tame, 'tis a pit-i-ful game.

word do they say, not a word do they say; With-out a sin-gle greet-ing they hur-ry a-way.

word do they say, not a word do they say; With-out a sin-gle greet-ing they hur-ry a-way.

f CHORUS OF KNIGHTS.

When at war, at his wine, on his steed.

CHORUS OF LADIES.

Our com - pa - ny they

do not ask.

Not a word do they say, With-

CHORUS OF KNIGHTS.

Know ye the knight by val - iant deed? Love is tame, 'tis a pit - ti - ful game,

Know ye the knight by val - iant deed?

-out a sin - gle greeting, They hur - ry a - way; De - ni - al is an ea - sy task, an ea - sy

-out a sin - gle greeting, They hur - ry a - way; De - ni - al is an ea - sy task, an ea - sy

When at war, at his wine, on his steed,

Love is tame, 'tis a pi - ti - ful game. When at war, at his wine, on his steed,

CHORUS OF LADIES.   **CHORUS OF KNIGHTS.**   **CHORUS**

task. Our com - pa - ny they do not ask. Know ye a knight by val - iant deed? Our

task. Our com - pa - ny they do not ask. Know ye a knight by val - iant deed? Our

86

I'LL WAIT NO LONGER.

No. 8. DUETT.

Andantino.

ASTOLF.

I'll wait.... no lon - ger, For love.... is stronger than word.... or vow.

I'll wait.... no lon-ger, For love.... is stronger that word or vow, than word or vow. This pride con-tending, Can have but one ending, To nature must bow,........ na - - ture must bow.

HELEN.

I'll wait .... no lon-ger, For love.... is stronger than word or vow.

I'll wait.... no lon-ger, For love.... is stronger than word or vow, than

word or vow. This pride con-tending, Can have but one ending, To na-ture must bow,........ Na - - ture must bow.

HELEN.

A - - stolf!

HELEN.   ASTOLF.   HELEN.

A - stolf!   Do   not   flee   me!   Shall   I

fp
Astolf.
stay,.... Or shall I go?...... Hel - - en,
how I've longed .... to see thee!
Helen.
No, I
can - - not, I can - - not leave him so, I can - not leave him
so, I can - not leave him so!
Astolf.
Ah, how I've longed to see thee!
cres.
p
f

Allegro vivace.

Tho' du - ty move, To keep my

Tho' du - ty move,

p

fp

fp

vow, So strong is love, I

To keep my vow, So strong is love,

fp

fp

can - not go, Pru - dence calls me back - ward,

I can - not go. Pru - dence

Flee, this sweet un-rest; For-ward, plead af-

calls me back-ward; Flee, this sweet un-rest, For-ward,

-fec-tion, Fall up-on his breast!

plead af-fec-tion, Fall up-on her breast!

Tho' du-ty move, To keep my

Tho' du-ty move,

vow, So strong is love, I
To keep my vow, So strong is love,
can - - not go, So strong is love,
I can - - not go, I can - - not
cresc.
Pru - dence calls me back - ward. Flee, this sweet un-
go. Pru - dence calls me back - ward,

rest; For - ward, pleads af - - fec - tion, Fall up -

Flee, this sweet un - rest; For - ward, pleads af - - fec - tion, Fall up -

- on his breast! Fall up - on his breast!

- on her breast! Fall up - on her breast!

Fall up - - on his breast!

Fall up - - on.................. her breast!

THRO' DANGERS I'VE GONE.

No. 9. ARIETTE.

Allegro Moderato.

COUNT.

Thro' dan-gers I've gone, And long was I fight-ing for thee, for thee; With hard-ships un-known my-self was re-quit-ing for thee, for thee; And thirst en-dured, ma-ny days not eat-en, for thee, for thee, A hun - dred, at least, of Turks I have beat - en

For thee, for thee ; My life and my blood I have

risked in these quar - rels, For thee for.......... thee ; Now

home - ward I come all cov - ered with lau - rels, For thee, for......... thee, Thro' dan - gers I've gone and long was I fight - ing, With hard - ships un-

- known my- self was re- quit - ing; And thirst en- dured, ma-ny days not eat - en, A

hun - dred, at least, of Turks I have beat - en. My life and my blood I have risked in these quar - rels, My life I have risked in these quar - rels, Now home - ward I come, all

cov - ered with lau - rels For thee, for......... thee, Now home - ward I

come all cov - ered with lau - rels For thee, for......... thee,

for thee,........ for thee..................

THOU WAST FIGHTING FOR ME.

No. 10. ARIETTE.

Allegro Moderato.

COUNTESS.

Sup-pose, then, that real-ly so long thou wast fight-ing, For me, for, me, With hun-ger and hard-ship thy-self wast re-quit-ing, For me, for me, 'Tis all good for naught, Such a war-like dis-po-si-tion, For me, for me, A life of peace were a reas-on-able con-di - tion.

For me, for me. And since for hon - or e-nough thou hast

striv - en, For me, for............ me, 'Tis fair that thy

life now to love be giv - en, For me, for........ .. me. Sup -

-pose then that real - ly so long thou wast fight - ing, With hun - ger and hard - ship thy-
-self wast re-quit - ing. 'Tis all good for naught, such a war-like dis-po-si - tion; A
life of peace were a reas-on-able con-di - tion. And since for hon - or e-
cres.
fp
-nough thou hast striv - en, Since for hou - or e-nough thou hast striv - en, 'Tis
fp

fair that thy life now to love be giv - en, For me, for......

me, 'Tis fair that thy life now to love be giv - en, For me,

for...... me, for me,...... for me!...............

No. 11. FINALE.

Allegro giusto.

COUNT.

How!

Can I trust my ver - y eyes?   In arm - or!

What a sweet sur - prise!   In arm - or?

What a sweet sur - prise!   Come hith - er, all ye knights, to me!   Come

fz fz fz fz

hith - er, all ye knights to me! The val - or of our la - - dies
see. Tho' pride was sore - ly test - ed, From
CHORUS OF KNIGHTS.
Tho' pride was sore - ly test - ed, From us the vic - to - ry was
p
fz
us the vic - t'ry was wrest - ed. It is the hap - - piest lot on earth, Of
wrest - ed. It is the hap - - piest lot........ on earth, Of

woman's love to know the worth, It is the hap - - piest

woman's love to know the worth, It is the hap - - piest

lot on earth......... Of wo - man's love to know the worth.

lot on earth, Of wo - man's love to know the worth.

COUNTESS.

But

with your kind per - mis - - sion, Ap-pear - - an-ces de-ceive you, And

I must make th'admis - - - sion. Pray, ca - - va-liers, be-lieve me, That not in hope to please you, In jest,..... 'twas but in jest...... In coat of mail I had me dressed. It is...... not wo - man's stuff, Quick, let me cast it off. O cast it not a - side! fair

COUNT.

charm - er, Thou art so won-der - ful in ar - mor.

O cast it not a - side, fair

Chorus of Knights.

O cast it not a - side, fair

Countess.

Thou art so won-der - ful in ar - mor. Of

charm - er, ... Thou art so won-der - ful in ar - mor.

charm - er, ... Thou art so won-der - ful in ar - mor.

shame sure I shall die. If this the oth - er la - dies
COUNT.
O cast it not a-side, fair charm - er, Thou
cast it not a-side, fair charm - er, Thou art so won-der - ful in
cast it not a-side, fair charm - er, Thou art so won-der - ful in
spy. They prom - - ised me their
art so won - der-ful in ar - mor, Thou art so .... won - der-
ar - mor, O cast it not a - side, fair charm - er, Thou art so won - der-
ar - mor, O cast it not a - side, fair charm - er, Thou art so won - der-

110

shame sure I shall die. If this the oth - er la - dies

won - der - ful in ar - mor, Thou art so won - der - ful in

art so won-der - ful in

spy...................

ar - - - mor.

ar - - - mor.

_pp_

COUNTESS.

What hear I?

Ah, Ah me, I per - ish! For they have kept their word I know, While

I a - lone have broke my vow. Ah, Ah me, I per - ish!

cresc. poco a poco.

for they have kept their word I know, While I a - lone have broke my vow.

CHORUS OF LADIES. *(Armed with breast-plate, helmet, shield and spear, Helen leads them on.)*

HELEN. LUITGARD.

All the fears and

CAMILLA.

weak con - di - tion, Which a wo - man's lot be - tide, All of them we

cast a - side. War a - lone is our am - bi - tion, All of them we cast a - side, War a - lone is our am - bi - tion.

All the fears and weak con - di - tion, All of them we

cast a - side. War a - lone is our am - bi - tion, War a - lone is

CHORUS OF LADIES.

our am - bi - tion. To war, a - way no long - er stay, Where dangers press with la - test breath, We'll

fol - low you to life or death! To war a - way. No

lon - ger stay, Where dan - gers press, with la - test breath, We'll fol - low you to life or death!

COUNTESS. *(forgetting that she herself is in armor.)*

In ar-mor ye? but tell me how! In ar-mor ye? but tell me how!

CHORUS OF LADIES.

Pray! do be-think ye of your vow! Pray! do be-think ye of your vow! Our

mod-el thou (O la-dy dear), Thou bear'st thy-self both shield and spear, Thou bear'st   thy - self both shield   and spear, Bear'st thy - self both shield and spear.

Andante.
COUNTESS. (*Aside.*)

I am chagrined.   By this unforeseen ad - venture,   I've lost my right to cen-

CHORUS OF LADIES.

She is chagrined.   By this unforeseen ad - venture,   She's lost her right to cen-

CHORUS OF KNIGHTS.   They are chagrined.   Let eve - ry knight,

Andante.

- sure. I made the vow, I did de - mand.
- sure. She made the vow, She did de - mand.
To pun - ish his sweet charm - er, With grace now lay a - side, a - side his
And now in ar - mor here I stand. I am chagrined.
And now in ar - mor she doth stand. She is chagrined.
ar - mor. And now in ar - mor there they stand. They are cha-

by this un-forseen ad - venture, I've lost my right to cen - sure;

by this un-forseen ad - venture, She's lost the right to cen - sure;

- grined, Let ev'-ry knight, To pun - ish his sweet charm-

I made the vow, I did de - mand, And now in ar - mor here I

She made the vow, She did de - mand, And there in ar - mor she doth

- er, With grace now lay a - side, A - side this ar - - mor;

stand; I am cha - grined, I made the
stand; She is cha - grined, She made the
And now in ar-mor there they stand; They are chagrined, Now doff our ar - - mor,
vow, And here I stand in ar - mor, in ar - mor.
vow, And she doth stand in ar - mor, in ar - mor.
Now doff our ar - mor, Now doff, doff our ar - - - mor.
f
pp
fz

Tempo I.　　　　　　　　　　　　　　HELEN.

What ye de - sired has hap - - pened now.

There-from the might............ of love ye know,

There-from the might of love.... ...... ye

COUNT.

know. By all the Ce - dars of Le - banon, More dan - gerous foe we nev - er met, To fail, would have fill'd us with re - gret, To fail, would have fill'd us with re -

- gret ; For tho' we have con - quered, Our hearts are

wou!

Andantino. ASTOLF *and* GAROLD.

FREDERIC *and the other* KNIGHTS.

When cour - age is to

Andantino.

124

beau - ty joined, What moot the val - or of a knight? Ye're on - ly to ap - pear, to con-quer, For

all.... are van - quished, are van - quished at the sight; Now fol - low, com - rades. Our ex-

- am - ple, Be - fore the fair - est of the fair, Lay down your arms, and with us

hast - en, Your knight - ly hom - age to of - fer there, Your knightly hom - age to of - fer there.

mf Chorus of Knights.

As prisoners, com - rades, now sur - ren - der, Be - fore the fair - est of the fair, Down in the dust your weap - ons lay ye, Your knight - ly hom - age of - fer

COUNTESS.

there, Your hom-age of-fer there.

Thro' love I

COUNT.

And ye? and ye?

too am weak, Ye have the revenge ye seek. To-day shall be the feast of love, To-

Tempo I. CHORUS OF KNIGHTS.

-mor-row on to bat-tle move. Hur-rah! hur-rah! the vic-to-ry is ours!

Tempo I.

mf *f* *fz* *p*

COUNT.

No more war,.... give........ me thy hand. No more war, We will not leave our na - tive land. My faith - ful page informed me

tru - ly, Ye had a lit - tle plan arranged, By which our life should now be

changed. I learned in time to........ spoil it du - ly, By coun - ter - plot. And

Know ye not, From home we nev - - er more would turn ? Ye

la - - dies should from us now learn........ It be - seems a wo - man

not to gain her wish by op-po - si - tion; By gra - cious mien and

ten - derness, These are a wo - mans' sweet tra - di - tion, By gra - cious mien and ten - derness, These are a wo-man's sweet tra - di-tion. Thee, U - do - lin, for du - ty

cres. *f* *p*

ISELLA.

done, I - sel - la's hand. 'Twas his long gone.

cres. *p* *cres.* *f*

Allegro moderato. CHORUS OF KNIGHTS.

Seek not, la - dies, strong - er weap - ons, When your Knights ye would dis-

Seek not, la - dies, strong - er weap - ons, When your Knights ye would dis-

Allegro moderato.

p

arm, Than the weap-ons na - ture gave you, Love and ten - der - ness your

- arm, Than the weap - ons na - ture gave you, Love and ten - der - ness your

charm. Seek not, la - dies, strong-er weap-ons, When your Knights ye would dis - arm, Than the

charm. Seek not, la - dies, strong-er weap-ons, When your Knights ye would dis - arm, Than the

weap-ons na - ture gave you, Love and ten - der-ness your charm, Love and ten - der-ness your

weap-ons na - ture gave you, Love and ten - der-ness your charm, Love and ten - der-ness your

Chorus of Ladies.

Seek not, la - dies, strong - er wea - pons, When our knights we would dis-

charm, When your knights ye would dis-

arm, Than the wea - pons na - ture gave us, Love and ten - der - ness, our

arm, Love and ten - der - ness your

charm. When our knights we would dis-arm.

charm. Seek not, la - dies, strong - er wea - pons, When your knights ye would dis - arm, Than the

Love and ten - derness our charm, Love and ten - derness our

wea - pons na - ture gave you, Love and ten - der-ness, your charm, Love and ten - der-ness your charm ev - er, ev - er love and ten - - - der-ness, our

charm ev - er, ev - er love and ten - - der-ness, your

charm.

charm.

INDEX.

J. Frank Giles, Music Typographer, 266 Washington St., Boston.

www.ingramcontent.com/pod-product-compliance
Lightning Source LLC
Chambersburg PA
CBHW030611270326
41927CB00007B/1120